I love YOU

summersdale

I LOVE YOU

Summersdale Publishers Ltd
46 West Street
Chichester
West Sussex
PO19 1RP
UK

www.summersdale.com

Printed and bound in Croatia

ISBN: 978-1-78685-227-4

Substantial discounts on bulk quantities of Summersdale books are available to corporations, professional associations and other organisations. For details contact general enquiries: telephone: +44 (0) 1243 771107 or email: enquiries@summersdale.com.

TO.....................

FROM..................

MY LOVE
IS SUCH
THAT
RIVERS
CANNOT
QUENCH.

Anne Bradstreet

I LOVE THEE
WITH THE BREATH,
SMILES, TEARS, OF
ALL MY LIFE.

Elizabeth Barrett Browning

MY HEART HAS
MADE ITS MIND UP
AND I'M AFRAID
IT'S YOU.

Wendy Cope

you MAKE
my day all
year ROUND.

LOVE IS THE
STRONGEST FORCE
THE WORLD POSSESSES.

MAHATMA GANDHI

IF I WERE TO
LIVE A THOUSAND YEARS,
I WOULD BELONG
TO YOU FOR ALL
OF THEM.

Michelle Hodkin

LOVE IS
THE ONLY SANE AND
SATISFACTORY ANSWER
TO THE PROBLEM OF
HUMAN EXISTENCE.

Erich Fromm

LET YOUR LOVE BE
LIKE THE MISTY RAINS,
COMING SOFTLY,
BUT FLOODING
THE RIVER.

Malagasy proverb

LOVE
MUST BE
AS MUCH
A LIGHT,
AS IT IS
A FLAME.

Henry David Thoreau

your HUGS are the BEST.

I WANT EVERYONE
TO MEET YOU. YOU'RE
MY FAVOURITE PERSON
OF ALL TIME.

Rainbow Rowell

LOVE IS
THE MAGICIAN
THAT PULLS MAN
OUT OF HIS
OWN HAT.

Ben Hecht

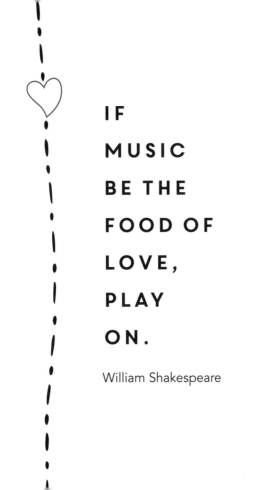

IF
MUSIC
BE THE
FOOD OF
LOVE,
PLAY
ON.

William Shakespeare

TAKE
MY HAND
AND DON'T
LET GO.

FALLING
IN LOVE COULD
BE ACHIEVED IN A
SINGLE WORD —
A GLANCE.

Ian McEwan

LOVE
MAKES
YOUR
SOUL
CRAWL
OUT FROM
ITS HIDING
PLACE.

Zora Neale Hurston

I LOVE YOU NOT
ONLY FOR WHAT YOU
ARE, BUT FOR WHAT
I AM WHEN I AM
WITH YOU.

Elizabeth Barrett Browning

**WE CAN ONLY
LEARN TO LOVE
BY LOVING.**

Iris Murdoch

I AM
always
HERE
FOR
YOU.

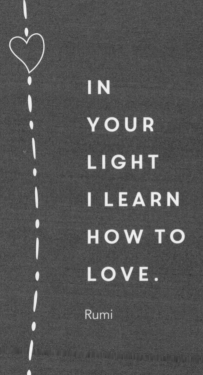

IN
YOUR
LIGHT
I LEARN
HOW TO
LOVE.

Rumi

YOU
are so
IMPORTANT
to me.

IF YOU
REMEMBER ME,
THEN I DON'T
CARE IF EVERYONE
ELSE FORGETS.

Haruki Murakami

ROMANCE IS
THE GLAMOUR WHICH
TURNS THE DUST OF
EVERYDAY LIFE INTO A
GOLDEN HAZE.

Elinor Glyn

SEIZE THE MOMENTS
OF HAPPINESS, LOVE
AND BE LOVED! THAT IS
THE ONLY REALITY
IN THE WORLD,
ALL ELSE IS FOLLY.

Leo Tolstoy

LOVE IS A
CANVAS FURNISHED
BY NATURE AND
EMBROIDERED BY
IMAGINATION.

Voltaire

SOMETIMES
THE HEART SEES
WHAT IS INVISIBLE
TO THE EYE.

H. JACKSON BROWN JR

I love being
IN LOVE
with YOU.

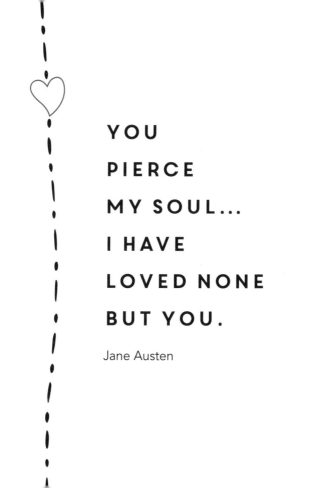

YOU
PIERCE
MY SOUL...
I HAVE
LOVED NONE
BUT YOU.

Jane Austen

DAY BY DAY
AND NIGHT BY NIGHT
WE WERE TOGETHER
— ALL ELSE HAS LONG
BEEN FORGOTTEN
BY ME.

Walt Whitman

LOVE IS THE
ONLY FLOWER
THAT GROWS AND
BLOSSOMS WITHOUT
THE AID OF THE
SEASONS.

Kahlil Gibran

IN YOU
I HAVE
FOUND MY
CLOSEST
FRIEND.

THE MOST PRECIOUS
POSSESSION THAT
EVER COMES TO A
MAN IN THIS WORLD IS
A WOMAN'S HEART.

Josiah Gilbert Holland

YOURS IS THE
LIGHT BY WHICH
MY SPIRIT'S BORN...
YOU ARE MY SUN,
MY MOON, AND
ALL MY STARS.

E. E. Cummings

**WHEN I SAW
YOU I FELL IN
LOVE, AND YOU
SMILED BECAUSE
YOU KNEW.**

Arrigo Boito

LOVE SHOULD
BE A TREE WHOSE
ROOTS ARE DEEP IN
THE EARTH, BUT WHOSE
BRANCHES EXTEND
INTO HEAVEN.

Bertrand Russell

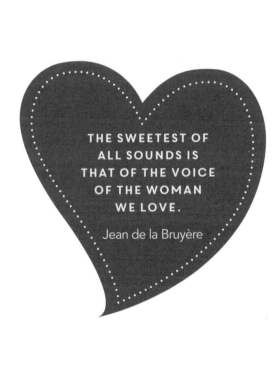

THE SWEETEST OF
ALL SOUNDS IS
THAT OF THE VOICE
OF THE WOMAN
WE LOVE.

Jean de la Bruyère

Together
we are
UNSTOPPABLE.

I AM IN
YOU AND YOU
IN ME, MUTUAL IN
DIVINE LOVE.

WILLIAM BLAKE

**THE SIMPLE
LACK OF HER
IS MORE TO ME
THAN OTHERS'
PRESENCE.**

Edward Thomas

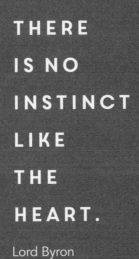

THERE
IS NO
INSTINCT
LIKE
THE
HEART.

Lord Byron

REMEMBER THAT
WHEREVER YOUR
HEART IS, THERE
YOU WILL FIND
YOUR TREASURE.

Paulo Coelho

your HUGS
are my
FAVOURITE
place.

LOVE IS
THE EMBLEM
OF ETERNITY.

Germaine de Staël

LOVE
BETTERS
WHAT
IS
BEST.

William Wordsworth

I LOVE YOU
TO ANOTHER
GALAXY AND
BACK.

LOVE TAKES
OFF MASKS THAT
WE FEAR WE CANNOT
LIVE WITHOUT AND
KNOW WE CANNOT
LIVE WITHIN.

James A. Baldwin

**WE DON'T
BELIEVE IN
RHEUMATISM
AND TRUE LOVE
UNTIL AFTER THE
FIRST ATTACK.**

Marie von Ebner-Eschenbach

MAY YOU LIVE AS
LONG AS YOU WISH
AND LOVE AS LONG
AS YOU LIVE.

Robert A. Heinlein

WE ARE ALL MORTAL
UNTIL THE FIRST KISS
AND THE SECOND
GLASS OF WINE.

Eduardo Galeano

OUR BEST
CONVERSATIONS
ARE WITHOUT
WORDS.

**LOVE IS
THE ONLY GOLD.**

Alfred, Lord Tennyson

GROW OLD
ALONG WITH ME!
THE BEST IS
YET TO BE.

ROBERT BROWNING

HOLD on to my HEART and keep it SAFE.

**IN DREAMS
AND IN LOVE
THERE ARE NO
IMPOSSIBILITIES.**

János Arany

IT IS
IMPOSSIBLE
TO LOVE
AND TO
BE WISE.

Francis Bacon

**LOVE IS
WHEN YOU MEET
SOMEONE WHO TELLS
YOU SOMETHING NEW
ABOUT YOURSELF.**

André Breton

HERE ARE FRUITS,
FLOWERS, LEAVES AND
BRANCHES, AND THEN
HERE IS MY HEART,
WHICH BEATS ONLY
FOR YOU.

Paul Verlaine

Love
MAKES
US
RICHER.

LOVE
KEEPS THE
COLD OUT
BETTER
THAN A
CLOAK.

Henry Wadsworth Longfellow

WHEN
YOU LOVE
SOMEONE, ALL
YOUR SAVED-UP
WISHES START
COMING OUT.

Elizabeth Bowen

●-■-●-■-●-■-●-■-●-■-●-■-●-■-●-■-●-■-●

YOU
ARE LIKE
A HOT
CHOCOLATE
ON A
RAINY DAY.

●-■-●-■-●-■-●-■-●-■-●-■-●-■-●-■-●-■-●

LOVERS ALONE
WEAR SUNLIGHT.

E. E. CUMMINGS

IN EVERY LIVING
THING THERE IS THE
DESIRE FOR LOVE.

D. H. Lawrence

You BRIGHTEN up my DARKEST days.

YOU ARE
ALWAYS NEW.
THE LAST OF YOUR
KISSES WAS EVER
THE SWEETEST.

John Keats

SO,
I LOVE YOU
BECAUSE THE
ENTIRE UNIVERSE
CONSPIRED TO
HELP ME FIND
YOU.

Paulo Coelho

A COWARD
IS INCAPABLE OF
EXHIBITING LOVE; IT
IS THE PREROGATIVE
OF THE BRAVE.

Mahatma Gandhi

**O MY LUVE'S
LIKE THE MELODIE,
THAT'S SWEETLY
PLAY'D IN TUNE.**

Robert Burns

YOU MAKE ME FEEL SO *lucky.*

A HEART
THAT LOVES IS
ALWAYS YOUNG.

Greek proverb

TO LIVE
IS LIKE TO LOVE
— ALL REASON IS
AGAINST IT, AND
ALL HEALTHY
INSTINCT FOR IT.

Samuel Butler

WHAT

would I do

WITHOUT

you?

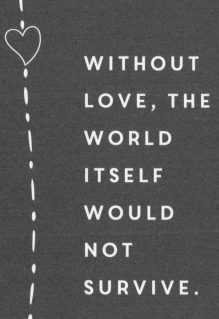

WITHOUT
LOVE, THE
WORLD
ITSELF
WOULD
NOT
SURVIVE.

Lope de Vega

ONE WORD
FREES US OF
ALL THE WEIGHT
AND PAIN OF LIFE:
THAT WORD
IS LOVE.

Sophocles

I KISSED A LOT
OF FROGS AND NOW
I'VE FOUND MY PRINCE.

JOAN COLLINS

LOVE DOES NOT
CONSIST OF GAZING
AT EACH OTHER BUT IN
LOOKING OUTWARD
TOGETHER IN THE
SAME DIRECTION.

Antoine de Saint-Exupéry

We are
TWO
HALVES
of one
WHOLE.

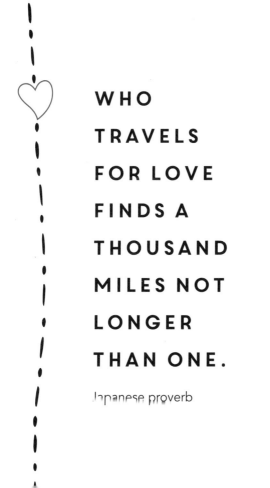

WHO
TRAVELS
FOR LOVE
FINDS A
THOUSAND
MILES NOT
LONGER
THAN ONE.

Japanese proverb

I WAS MADE AND
MEANT TO LOOK FOR
YOU AND WAIT FOR
YOU AND BECOME
YOURS FOREVER.

Robert Browning

YOU ARE MY *favourite* PERSON.

THERE ARE
ALL KINDS OF LOVE
IN THIS WORLD BUT
NEVER THE SAME
LOVE TWICE.

F. Scott Fitzgerald

**LOVE IS
THE WISDOM
OF THE FOOL
AND THE
FOLLY OF
THE WISE.**

Samuel Johnson

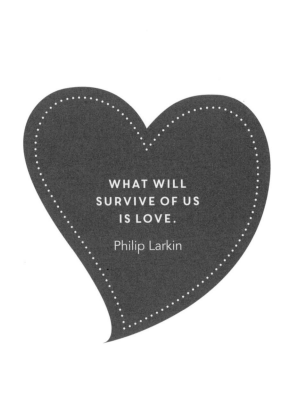

WHAT WILL
SURVIVE OF US
IS LOVE.

Philip Larkin

**MAKE ME
IMMORTAL
WITH A KISS.**

Christopher Marlowe

I LOVE
YOU MORE
THAN THERE
ARE STARS
IN THE SKY.

**LOVE SHALL
BE OUR TOKEN,
LOVE BE YOURS
AND LOVE
BE MINE.**

Christina Rossetti

I CAN
DO ANYTHING
WITH YOU BY
MY SIDE.

**LOVE IS
SOMETHING ETERNAL;
THE ASPECT MAY CHANGE,
BUT NOT THE ESSENCE.**

Vincent van Gogh

**THEY SAY LOVE IS
THE BEST INVESTMENT;
THE MORE YOU GIVE,
THE MORE YOU GET
IN RETURN.**

Audrey Hepburn

LOVE
IS THE
GREATEST
REFRESHMENT
IN LIFE.

Pablo Picasso

IF NOTHING SAVES US FROM DEATH, AT LEAST LOVE SHOULD SAVE US FROM LIFE.

Pablo Neruda

LOVE
CONQUERS
ALL.

Virgil

You and
me were

MEANT
TO BE.

**A KISS IS
A LOVELY TRICK
DESIGNED BY NATURE
TO STOP SPEECH WHEN
WORDS BECOME
SUPERFLUOUS.**

Ingrid Bergman

LOVE DISCOVERS TRUTHS
ABOUT INDIVIDUALS
THAT OTHERS
CANNOT SEE.

Søren Kierkegaard

YOU
ARE
MY
happy
PLACE.

LOVE IS
ALWAYS
BEFORE YOU.

ANDRÉ BRETON

IT'S THE
KIND OF KISS THAT
INSPIRES STARS TO
CLIMB INTO THE SKY
AND LIGHT UP
THE WORLD.

Tahereh Mafi

LOVE IS
THE ONE THING
STRONGER THAN
DESIRE AND THE
ONLY PROPER
REASON TO RESIST
TEMPTATION.

Jeanette Winterson

TWO SOULS ARE
SOMETIMES CREATED
TOGETHER AND...
IN LOVE BEFORE
THEY'RE BORN.

F. Scott Fitzgerald

EVERY
DAY *with*
you is an
ADVENTURE.

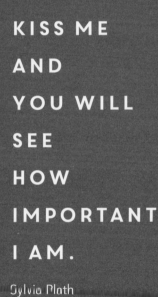

KISS ME
AND
YOU WILL
SEE
HOW
IMPORTANT
I AM.

Sylvia Plath

WHEN
LOVE EXISTS,
NOTHING ELSE
MATTERS.

Isabel Allende

YOU
MAKE MY
HEART SING,
AND IT'S SUCH
A SWEET
MELODY.

**LOVE BRINGS
LIGHT TO A LOVER'S
NOBLE AND HIDDEN
QUALITIES – HIS RARE
AND EXCEPTIONAL
TRAITS.**

Friedrich Nietzsche

LOVE IS NOT
CONSOLATION.
IT IS LIGHT.

SIMONE WEIL

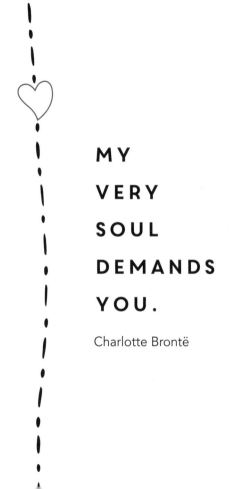

MY
VERY
SOUL
DEMANDS
YOU.

Charlotte Brontë

**A KISS MAKES
THE HEART
YOUNG AGAIN
AND WIPES OUT
THE YEARS.**

Rupert Brooke

Your smile
LIGHTS UP
a room.

**THE KISS ITSELF IS
IMMORTAL. IT TRAVELS
FROM LIP TO LIP,
CENTURY TO CENTURY,
FROM AGE TO AGE.**

Guy de Maupassant

YOU SHOULD
BE KISSED
OFTEN, AND BY
SOMEONE WHO
KNOWS HOW.

Margaret Mitchell

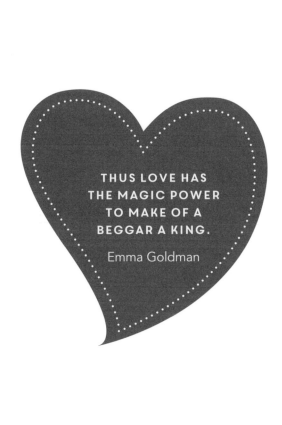

THUS LOVE HAS
THE MAGIC POWER
TO MAKE OF A
BEGGAR A KING.

Emma Goldman

YOU
are my
HOME.

THE ONE THING
WE CAN NEVER
GET ENOUGH
OF IS LOVE.

Henry Miller

YOU
ARE MY
HEART,
MY LIFE,
MY ONE
AND
ONLY
THOUGHT.

Arthur Conan Doyle

**A KISS ON THE
BEACH WHEN THERE
IS A FULL MOON IS
THE CLOSEST THING
TO HEAVEN.**

H. Jackson Brown Jr

THERE IS
NOTHING
WE CAN'T
TALK ABOUT
TOGETHER.

TRUE LOVE BELIEVES EVERYTHING, AND BEARS EVERYTHING, AND TRUSTS EVERYTHING.

Charles Dickens

THE PRAISE THAT
COMES FROM LOVE
DOES NOT MAKE
US VAIN, BUT
MORE HUMBLE.

J. M. Barrie

EVERYTHING
IN OUR LIFE
SHOULD BE BASED
ON LOVE.

RAY BRADBURY

LOVE WILL
FIND ITS WAY
THROUGH PATHS
WHERE WOLVES
WOULD FEAR
TO PREY.

Lord Byron

WHATEVER
OUR SOULS
ARE MADE OF,
HIS AND MINE
ARE THE
SAME.

Emily Brontë

YOU

ARE

perfect

TO

ME.

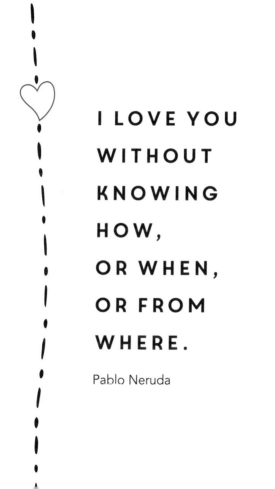

I LOVE YOU
WITHOUT
KNOWING
HOW,
OR WHEN,
OR FROM
WHERE.

Pablo Neruda

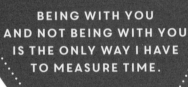

BEING WITH YOU
AND NOT BEING WITH YOU
IS THE ONLY WAY I HAVE
TO MEASURE TIME.

Jorge Luis Borges

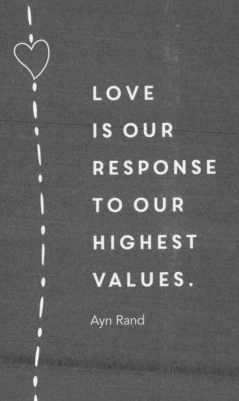

LOVE
IS OUR
RESPONSE
TO OUR
HIGHEST
VALUES.

Ayn Rand

LOVERS NEED TO
KNOW HOW TO
LOSE THEMSELVES
AND THEN HOW TO
FIND THEMSELVES
AGAIN.

Paulo Coelho

EVERY DAY
WE SPEND
TOGETHER IS
PRECIOUS.

**EARTH'S THE RIGHT
PLACE FOR LOVE:
I DON'T KNOW
WHERE IT'S LIKELY
TO GO BETTER.**

Robert Frost

LOVE'S TOO PRECIOUS TO BE LOST, A LITTLE GRAIN SHALL NOT BE SPILT.

Alfred, Lord Tennyson

you BRING me so much JOY.

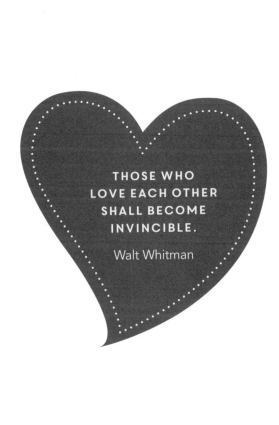

THOSE WHO
LOVE EACH OTHER
SHALL BECOME
INVINCIBLE.

Walt Whitman

LOVE HAS
ALWAYS BEEN THE
MOST IMPORTANT
BUSINESS IN MY LIFE;
I SHOULD SAY
THE ONLY ONE.

Stendhal

I AM IN LOVE
– AND, MY GOD,
IT'S THE GREATEST
THING THAT CAN
HAPPEN TO
A MAN.

D. H. Lawrence

I KNOW OF
ONLY ONE DUTY,
AND THAT IS
TO LOVE.

ALBERT CAMUS

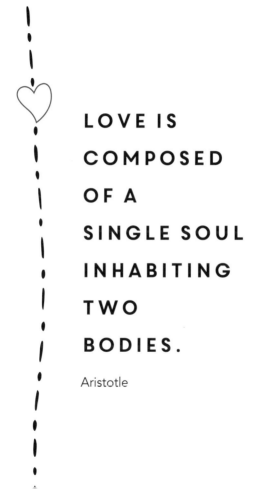

LOVE IS
COMPOSED
OF A
SINGLE SOUL
INHABITING
TWO
BODIES.

Aristotle

I LOVE
YOU IN
EVERY
LANGUAGE.

**HER LIPS ON HIS
COULD TELL HIM BETTER
THAN ALL HER
STUMBLING WORDS.**

Margaret Mitchell

OR LEAVE A KISS
BUT IN THE CUP,
AND I'LL NOT
LOOK FOR WINE.

Ben Jonson

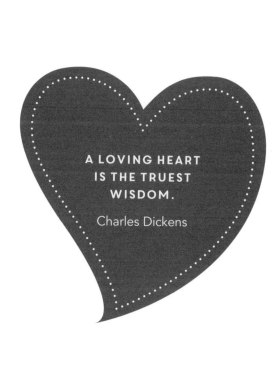

A LOVING HEART
IS THE TRUEST
WISDOM.

Charles Dickens

you MAKE
me a
BETTER
person.

THE SOUND
OF A KISS IS
NOT SO LOUD AS
THAT OF A CANNON,
BUT ITS ECHO
LASTS A GREAT
DEAL LONGER

Oliver Wendell Holmes Sr

LOVE IS OF
ALL PASSIONS
THE STRONGEST,
FOR IT ATTACKS
SIMULTANEOUSLY
THE HEAD, THE HEART
AND THE SENSES.

Lao Tzu

**TO WITNESS
TWO LOVERS IS
A SPECTACLE
FOR THE GODS.**

Johann Wolfgang von Goethe

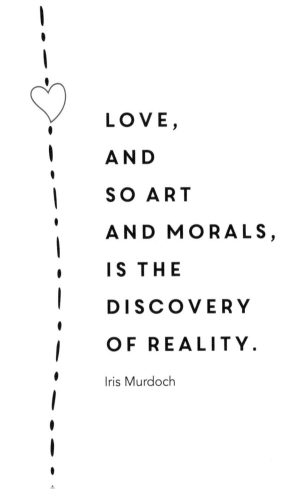

LOVE,
AND
SO ART
AND MORALS,
IS THE
DISCOVERY
OF REALITY.

Iris Murdoch

YOU

complete

ME.

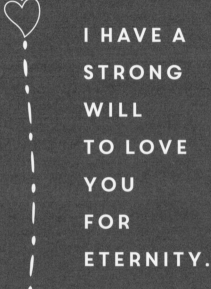

I HAVE A
STRONG
WILL
TO LOVE
YOU
FOR
ETERNITY.

Milan Kundera

IS NOT A KISS
THE VERY
AUTOGRAPH
OF LOVE?

HENRY THEOPHILUS FINCK

COME LIVE
IN MY HEART
AND PAY
NO RENT.

Samuel Lover

LET'S DO
EVERYTHING
ON EARTH
TOGETHER.

IN LOVE,
ONE AND ONE
ARE ONE.

Jean-Paul Sartre

BY MY SOUL,
I CAN NEITHER EAT,
DRINK, NOR SLEEP; NOR,
WHAT'S STILL WORSE,
LOVE ANY WOMAN
IN THE WORLD
BUT HER.

Samuel Richardson

WE LOVED WITH
A LOVE THAT WAS
MORE THAN LOVE.

EDGAR ALLAN POE

**ULTIMATELY,
LOVE IS
EVERYTHING.**

M. Scott Peck

I ASK YOU
TO PASS THROUGH
LIFE AT MY SIDE — TO
BE MY SECOND SELF,
AND BEST EARTHLY
COMPANION.

Charlotte Brontë

I
love
YOU.

If you're interested in finding out more
about our books, find us on Facebook at
Summersdale Publishers and follow
us on Twitter at **@Summersdale**.

www.summersdale.com